HOW TO COME UP WITH THE PASSIVE INCOME IDEAS

How to Use Your Current Activity As a Source of Passive Income

Donald Haskins

TABLE OF CONTENTS

INTRODUCTION

CHAPTER 1. WHAT IS A PASSIVE INCOME?

CHAPTER 2. TYPES OF PASSIVE INCOME

CHAPTER 3. USEFUL STEPS

    Starting Point

    Analysis

    Automatization and Delegation

    Maintenance and Diversification

CHAPTER 4. HOW DO I START?

    Activity

CHAPTER 5. MOVE YOUR WORK TO THE INTERNET – A MODERN SOURCE FOR PASSIVE INCOME

    Can You Make Video Courses for Your Customers?

    Can You Make Something Else?

    Do It by Yourself or Delegate It

    Sell It

    Or Invest and Buy It Ready

    Activity

CHAPTER 6. WHAT DO YOU HAVE? USE YOUR PROPERTY TO GENERATE PASSIVE INCOME

    Can You Use Your Photos to Get Passive Income?

    Can You Give Your Property for Rent?

    Sublease Somebody's Assets in an Activity

    Earn With P2P Lending

    Don't You Forget About The Simplest?

Activity

CHAPTER 7. IS IT POSSIBLE FOR YOU TO EARN MONEY WITH SOCIAL NETWORKS?

How Can You Use Your Account on Instagram to Make Money?

Activity

CONCLUSION

INTRODUCTION

Most people have a very common dream and desire – to earn money without working. Day by day, people try to build such a business and it really works for some.

There are 6 reasons why people aim to have a passive income, and they are very simple:

1. **Mobility and freedom** – you are free from the office area and it's your choice when to get up, when to have lunch and when to go to meet with your friends.

2. **Time** – you are the master of your time and do not depend on anyone in planning your activities.

3. **Independence** – having a passive income, you don't care about your salary, bonuses or schedule.

4. Safety – correctly organized and managed passive income can indemnity in a case of dismissal. You don't have to worry about your job and you don't have to be afraid of losing it.

5. Assured future – maybe not very distant future, but assured. Looking further, you can count at a wonderful and pleasant retirement, laying on the beach while money flows into your accounts.

6. Stability – the last, but not least. A well-built passive income is something that constantly brings you money, and this fact creates a personal island of financial stability.

If these 6 reasons motivate and push you to think about the creation of a personal business (or other assets) that would bring you passive income, then this book is definitely for you!

You can find advice and practical examples of how to start and what to know before starting here. Hope you will enjoy this book and that it will be useful to you.

Sincerely yours, Donald Haskins.

CHAPTER 1. WHAT IS A PASSIVE INCOME?

Passive income is one of the core terms in investment. It is closely related to financial freedom.

Passive income consists of revenues obtained without big effort and expenses from the investor's side. In short, you rest while money continues to come to your pocket. How is it possible?

The tip is to make your assets work for you and bring you passive income. There are many ideas of how to make money at home and it is up to each of us to choose the method most suitable for us.

The most appropriate words about passive income are those of J. Rockefeller's: "I would rather earn 1%

off a 100 people's efforts than 100% of my own efforts."

For generating a passive income, you need a way to maintain this income without working a lot to keep it going. If you have to work day by day to maintain the income, it means you have an active rather than passive income.

Passive income continues to flow, even when you don't make efforts daily. However, many forms of passive income still require daily or weekly activities, but it does not mean that you need to carry out these tasks by yourself.

You can delegate these tasks to other people, companies or _technologies_. For passive income to remain passive (that is, so you should not have to work hard to maintain cash flow), you need to remove the items from your to-do list, but these items still have to be performed.

CHAPTER 2. TYPES OF PASSIVE INCOME

Passive income means that you do something once and then earn a hundred times more from it.

For example, your intellectual knowledge and ideas can be considered as a source of earning – many people record some video lessons about something they know or pretend to know very well. The video lessons are recorded once and sold on the internet afterwards.

Other people live on income from properties or investments – they are called rentiers. From a financial point of view, 4 types of passive income can be distinguished:

- Investment income;

- Intellectual income;

- Marketing income;

- Legal income.

The first one, the investment income, encloses the real estates, bank accounts, equipment renting, etc.

The second one, the intellectual income, is based on the creation of an intellectual product (such as video lessons, practical courses, etc.) and its further selling. The passive income comes from an author's rights.

The third type of income, the marketing income, is connected with marketing – the most common example would be cosmetic companies that promote the creation of an internal structure with teams and pyramids. Also, a good option would be an internet site and advertising.

The last income, the legal one, is guaranteed by the government – benefits and facilities.

CHAPTER 3. USEFUL STEPS

Let's define the core steps that need to be done before getting a passive income.

First:

Starting Point

Start with thinking about the project and defining THE MAIN IDEA and THE TARGET. It is required to be morally ready to the fact that you'll need to work and make investments before you get any income. Make a plan with an estimation of costs. Define how much time you are ready to dedicate to the project and what is very important – your expectations.

Then you can proceed to the next step:

Analysis

Make an analysis of your potential. Make a list of what you have and what you need. This way, you'll have a clear picture of _the things you need and the things you already have_: experience in a certain field, knowledge, etc. Also, you can find information about projects similar to yours and read about them. This step is very important as it is the basement of your future actions.

Once you've set your plans, ideas and targets and analyzed them from all the points of view, it's time to start the project itself with one of the next steps:

Automatization and Delegation

These two important tools can help you in optimization and increasing efficiency. Depending on the field you want to develop your business in, you can use one or both.

For example, if you want to start an online business, you cannot do it without automatization. *Automatization expands the boundaries of any business* and increases its effectiveness a lot, especially if talking about the internet. Here, not using automatization is like having a car and pushing it instead of driving.

Automatization is a system which encloses a lot of important elements and a range of tools which are not very clear to everyone.

If you are not so initiated in the field, you can use the second tool, **delegation**. <u>A very important tip:</u> **The system of passive income is a form of delegation**. Important parts of your business in which you don't have the necessary skills are better off being delegated to professionals. This can be considered as an investment.

Generally, delegation is a very important tool and it can be used without automatization.

<u>To generate a passive income, you need **a method to maintain this income** without working too much</u>. Because, if you have to work a lot, it's an active rather than a passive income. However, many forms of passive income require some periodical actions. These actions can be delegated to other people and /or technologies.

To keep the income passive, you have to remove from your to-do list some points that can be done by other people or services. Delegation means rapidity, effectiveness, permanence and it is not expensive.

Well, once you've set your business up, you have nothing to do than to go to the next steps:

Maintenance and Diversification

Passive income doesn't mean you've done your work once and you can just stay and watch your money flow into your pocket. It has to be a well-built system which needs to be maintained systematically.

A good system gives good results. <u>Maintenance means constant improvement and innovation</u>. You have to always be sure that *the core tasks are done in time and that you have sufficient resources to sustain the business*.

At the same time, you have to be informed about the trends and new things that appear on the market. So, while other people or technicians work to keep your business going, you are thinking one step forward in order to assure a wise maintenance.

Not less important is diversification. This is also a desirable part of work in the passive income world. The only difference is that it is up to each owner whether they want to diversify or not. It can be done in different ways: by developing new ranges of business which can give you a feeling of safety.

It is good when risk diversification is present in a business. In case one business fails, you don't have to worry about your income as you have other businesses that still bring you passive cash flow.

Another way of diversification is an internal one. You can make internal changes in your business in order to keep up with the market requirements. This will help you keep your business stable and up to date.

All these are core things that everyone who wants to create a passive income should know.

However, this cannot be called a "finished picture" without concrete examples of how to start and what to do.

CHAPTER 4. HOW DO I START?

After reading a lot of things and definitions about passive income, an important question still continues to dominate your brains: "**How do I start?**"

The answer has three words that everyone who wants a passive income should know: ***simplification, automation and delegation***.

The question is, *do you have money to invest or to buy an asset*? Or *do you want to create an asset*? Or you have an asset and you just need to make it so it brings you passive income?

Depending on the answers to these questions, <u>you should plan your future actions</u>. I will just try to give you some push ideas and directions concerning options and tools to use.

In the next chapters, I would like to ask you several questions. Answering them will help you figure out how to obtain passive income from your activity.

Activity

Please, take a pencil and a piece of paper and write down what you have been doing before to earn money and what you are doing now. Then analyze the activities listed in the following chapters.

_____

_____

_____

_____

Hopefully it will be useful for you. I thought that you could use the space below each chapter to make some notes in case you need to.

CHAPTER 5. MOVE YOUR WORK TO THE INTERNET – A MODERN SOURCE FOR PASSIVE INCOME

The Internet has become a powerful tool in people's lives. It plays an important role as an informational resource, communication and also as a business platform.

The majority of people have access to the internet and for those who want not only to communicate, but also to make money, it is one of the cheapest and most perfect ways to do it.

Let's take an example. The easiest way to create a passive income is to make money from your knowledge. How? Very simple!

Can You Make Video Courses for Your Customers?

Possibly you can make some video courses - a good way to promote and use your knowledge. But maybe you can buy them along with the author's rights instead?

So, your knowledge is your asset in this case. You just have to think how to make a passive income. Worldwide, prices for video courses are very different, but on average, they are quite accessible.

The price generally varies between $20 and $200. Nowadays, video courses are very popular, people like them and they bring a good income.

Simplify and delegate making an asset to bring you passive income:

What is needed to create a video course?

The author tells about relevant and valuable skills and knowledge in which he is very good and experienced.

You don't need to spend time on individual lessons via Skype to earn money.

You just need to use the tools mentioned above: *simplify and delegate*.

Simplify by making it once and for good and then delegate for distribution.

Initially, a plan is needed for the content of the video. Remember one thing: you have to create something that will capture the public's interest. So you can make an analysis of what kind of video courses exist and decide what you can improve.

In a word, you can try to make something like a "*mystery shopper*" around the market and decide what you can do to make a difference.

After you've created your video, the next step is recording it on DVD and designing an attractive cover. Furthermore, you can either advertise it on your own by sending emails to your friends, or you can use social networks for advertising. You can also delegate this issue to someone else while you work on recording another video.

Meanwhile, *it would be great to think about a bonus system for the potential customers* and other things that can attract potential buyers. After you have the process set, you just have to maintain and diversify it. With a strong desire and some effort, this kind of passive income allows you to earn good money.

For example:

Approximate numbers: you have 20 000 emails. You can send proposals to buy your products for $20-$30 per one DVD. The DVD will be ordered by 1% of people and the payment will be made by around 145-150 people.

It means you will have sold 145-150 DVDs, somewhere $2900-4500. Take into consideration the postal costs for delivering – somewhere $500-1000.

In this way, your passive income will be somewhere between $200-3500, which is a quite good result. *A very good example is Derek Halpern's blog* – he tells about his own experience with video courses. It's a very nice and easy to understand story which can be very useful for those who want to take this path.

Can You Make Something Else?

1. You don't want to make video courses? Maybe, depending on your activity, **you could create a PDF course**?

2. If you have the skills and knowledge that you can share with others, why not to **create a closed forum with a monthly access fee or a group in one of the social networks**?

Very important: <u>create a referral program with generous royalties</u> which could help you attract professionals that work with internet traffic. For example, this is how the most famous authors do it: they give them 50-60% of income from each sale and they can count on tens and hundred daily sales of their product in return.

3. Maybe you should think about buying an email database for distribution. Periodically advertising through these emails, you can count on a certain response and result.

4. Can you make money on YouTube, showing your work?

Another way of getting a passive income via the Internet is YouTube. Everyone knows what YouTube is, but few are those who know that it can help you in getting a passive income. It is an amazing example of passive income. You just have to turn on your brains and make some effort. *But I have to remind you – you should delegate all the possible tasks to others!*

Make interesting movies and automatize the process to get reviews:

If you like to make short, interesting clips or short movies, you have the chance to make some money on YouTube! However, there is a BUT: you have to be patient because really good money will start to flow into your pocket only when your videos are watched by hundreds and thousands of people.

At this step, the advertisers will come to you, offering to pay you money for placing their advertisement several seconds before your short video.

Delegate the tasks to others if you need help:

At the same time, do not forget to place Google advertising – Google Adsense on your video page. If you are not informed well enough about this, you can easily delegate this issue to someone who is initiated in this field.

If you don't find anyone or you want to do it by yourself, you just have to google how to do it. You can read some information about Adsense by clicking on the following link: (https://support.google.com/adsense/answer/3180977?hl=en).

Another tip would be the possibility to earn on video previews. You can read about this site on the internet: (http://www.lifehack.org/articles/money/11-creative-ways-make-money-youtube.html). It is similar to YouTube. More detailed information on http://www.wikihow.com/Earn-Money-on-YouTube.

5. You can make money on websites, describing products, advertising providers and leaving feedback about your work:

Another source of passive income through the internet can be websites. It is enough to know several marketing tips, good PC knowledge and a big desire to work and you can start. Let's not forget that every project requires an investment of time and patience.

Do It by Yourself or Delegate It

For example, for reaching an amount of 1000 dollars per month from an internet site, it can take from 6 months to 2 years of developing and improving with several hours of work per day.

The main thing here is to understand that, if you want to make money, you have to invest time and effort; only after that can you count on some passive income. Once you've established the basement, you have nothing to do but delegate the administration of the web site's maintenance.

Sell It

<u>What else can you do with this asset?</u> It is very simple! An internet site which already brings stable income can be sold for an amount of 20 times more than its monthly income.

So, in this way, there are 2 ways of making assets which will bring you passive income: making internet sites, developing and maintaining them for constant future revenues or making internet sites for sale.

Let's not forget about the marketing – on this site, different advertisements and teasers can be placed which mean additional passive income.

Or Invest and Buy It Ready

If you are not very interested in developing a website or you are not very initiated in IT staff, but you have a certain amount of money ready to invest, you can simply buy an already active website. For this, though, you have to at least have an idea about this or the easy thing to do would be to delegate this to a specialist who will help you with maintenance and automatization.

Anyway, you'll need a site administrator and somebody who will work on the content. I would advise this to you only after you've managed to create your own website.

Activity

After reading this chapter, ask yourself if you have **someone in your activity who already managed to create a passive income**? What can you learn from their experience?

And for example – *can you apply the tools listed below to your activity*?

- Create and sell video courses about your activity:

_____

_____

_____

- Create and sell printed samples:

_____

_____

_____

- Create a closed forum or group on a social network:

_____

_____

_____

- Start to earn in a passive manner by selling your abilities through YouTube:

_____

_____

_____

- Start earning passive income by selling your abilities and experience on your web site/blog:

_____

_____

_____

Do you have any other thoughts after reading this chapter? Make some notes!

CHAPTER 6. WHAT DO YOU HAVE? USE YOUR PROPERTY TO GENERATE PASSIVE INCOME

What do you think of when you hear the word "property"? Of course, it is obvious that most people understand the term as a real estate, a car, some equipment and so on. From these types of properties, it is pretty clear how to obtain an income.

<u>What kind of properties do you have? What can you give for rent? Maybe you can create some digital assets?</u> Did you ever think that your photos, as your property, can also bring you some income? Yes, they can!

Can You Use Your Photos to Get Passive Income?

So, your asset – your photos. Here you do not need automatization or delegation. You can do everything by yourself. For this, the most suitable platforms are Shutterstock and iStockphoto.

I'll tell you about Shutterstock – the best photo bank nowadays where photographers start to earn the second they register. The platform has one secret – fresh photos are prioritized here.

That's why your pictures will be on top at first and you will earn money. Also, if the photo is downloaded many times, it becomes popular, which also increases the chance to increase the income.

Make high-quality photos and that's all:

The photos have to be JPG format, minimal size – 4 megapixels and some more requirements you have to follow while submitting your photos.

You can earn from $0.25 per photo – maybe it looks funny before thinking about the fact that one photo can be sold hundreds of times.

The amount changes, and you are not doing anything. So you can spend a little time to upload some images and get an additional passive income.

Can You Give Your Property for Rent?

Let's not forget about real property that can definitely bring you passive income. The essence of this method getting passive income is pretty clear at the first sight.

Delegate legal and organizational questions to professionals to avoid further misunderstandings:

Actually, this field has a lot of shades like:

- To give the place for a long or short period of time?

- How much revenue will it generate?

- How many expenses will you have?

- Risk that your property could be damaged

- Can you trust agencies to find clients for you?

- What taxes will you have to pay?

So, if you take into consideration all these things, you can proceed to give your property for rent. I think that this is the most understandable way of creating a passive income, as having a property means you already have a good asset.

If you don't have one, you have to invest to buy it. In a word, if you can afford to initiate such a business, go ahead and do it. *You can give for rent your house, your car or maybe you have some equipment or a garage you don't use.*

You don't need to make a big effort. Just advertise your proposal and wait. You can use delegation to ask somebody to find a customer for you. Depending on your asset, you have a lot of options!

Sublease Somebody's Assets in an Activity

Why won't you sublease somebody's assets in an activity you are experienced in? <u>Why not sell additional services?</u>

I'm sure you're quite experienced in your line and have already studied your target audience. Think about _what else you could propose to them_.

What can you buy for cheap and sell to the clients with a markup? What will they buy from you *just because it will be comfortable and accessible for them*?

Earn With P2P Lending

Let's suppose that you have money, but you don't want to invest it in buying real estates, equipment and other stuff like that. You just want your money to make money while you sleep.

So, good news! There is such possibility with P2P lending. With enough knowledge and wise risk assessment, you can give loans and earn money.

Make the process simple and choose the intermediator that will invest your money:

What is P2P? It means peer-to-peer when one person offers loans to other people without going to a bank.

You give a certain amount of money and after a certain period of time, you receive your money plus interest. But it is easy to say and hard to start.

What guarantees do you have? Will you receive your money back? These are the first important questions that usually come up. There are a lot of options to choose from for an intermediator. The most known one is Web transfer or Prosper.com.

I liked Jeremy Noel Johnson's post about Prosper.com and I advise you to read it. It has a lot of useful and important information. Also, this information is valuable because it was taken from his own experience. You can find it here: www.jeremynoeljohnson.com/investing/.

Don't You Forget About The Simplest?

What about the simplest? Open one more saving or deposit account

If you have money, but you don't feel safe investing in buying a real estate or in loans, the simplest and safest method for you to get some passive income is to open a saving or a deposit account in a bank.

This does not require your actions at all except going to the bank and signing an agreement. You just wait to get your money monthly.

You already have a saving or a deposit account?

It's good – *if you have available sources, open one more account*. *It is better than losing them because of inflation.*

Activity

Let's make a sum-up of the chapter. Think about **what you have at the moment and what you can add to your current activity to earn passive income**:

- Can you give your property for rent? Real estate, car, equipment, service?

_____

_____

_____

- Can you create digital assets from your activity? Maybe somebody would be interested in some photos of your professional activity?

_____

_____

_____

- Can you offer additional values that can be bought cheap and sold with a mark-up to your target audience?

_____

_____

_____

- Can you take part in P2P lending?

_____

_____

_____

- If you have money that is under risk to lose its value, why not open a bank account?

_____

_____

_____

Do you have any other thoughts after reading this chapter? Make some notes!

_____

_____

_____

_____

_____

_____

_____

_____

_____

_____

CHAPTER 7. IS IT POSSIBLE FOR YOU TO EARN MONEY WITH SOCIAL NETWORKS?

Have you ever thought about how Mark Zuckerberg and Pavel Durov became famous?

These two guys developed 2 of the most known social networks in the world – Facebook and VKontakte. "These guys really make huge money" you would say. And you are definitely right. Now they really have a passive income due to their business.

How Can You Use Your Account on Instagram to Make Money?

Actually, I'm not going to propose you to invent something like Facebook or Instagram or any other social network. I will offer you a method you can use to acquire passive income by using these social networks instead.

Promote your account and make money:

One of the most famous websites is Instagram. Millions and millions of people use this social network each month. This is why there is a chance to make money there. It is considered that Instagram is one of the most popular platforms for business development because of three reasons:

1. The information is transmitted on a visual basis;

2. The images are more effective in transmitting emotions and feelings than texts;

3. Emotions and feelings are the things that make your business here to go on.

So, let's see how to make a passive income with Instagram. The easiest way to start making money is to become popular.

It means you must have an account with many followers and you'll be able to advertise everything you are proposed – new brands, restaurants and many other things that you will be paid for.

You have to acquire somewhere around 100 000 followers to be a potential platform for advertisers. Here we come to the most important question, how to obtain all these followers? The answer is simple and not very simple – to promote!

Do it by yourself or delegate it to somebody:

The powerful internet offers you some ways of promotion:

a) Mass following – you subscribe to different accounts and you can count on a vice versa result for your Instagram. You can do this manually or by using different tools for automatization. You just have to ensure that your Instagram is interesting enough to receive reciprocity in subscribing.

b) Liking – it is similar to the mass following but you do not subscribe, you just "like" photos and you have a chance to receive "likes" back.

c) Spam – nobody likes it, but it works. You can leave comments to other users' photos and receive visitors on your account. You can even invite them to be your subscribers. If you are not blocked, it can work.

d) Advertising – the simplest method, but it implies additional costs. You must buy advertising space via

Facebook and different websites. You will receive likes, shares and subscribers as a result.

You can also hire somebody to promote your account if you feel like you are not very initiated in this stuff, but be ready for additional costs. Choosing an option is up to you. You'll get a result anyway. What's important is to understand that you can get also a bad result sometimes, which doesn't mean a failure.

It just means that you should change something in your actions. I would recommend reading *Jenn Herman's article "6 Tips to Grow Your Instagram Audience Quickly".*

Activity

After reading this chapter, answer the following questions:

- How can you advertise your activity through social networks?

_____

_____

_____

- How can you sell someone's products and services for a fee from the sales?

_____

_____

_____

- Do you know that there are special programs - bots that can execute some actions on a schedule basis, which can be used as advertising in a passive manner to attract users and transform them into potential buyers?

_____

_____

_____

- Imagine that you've found such a program and bought it – what could you sell with its help without investing your presence and having an almost automatic basis?

_____

_____

_____

Do you have any other thoughts after reading this chapter? Make some notes!

CONCLUSION

Dear fellows, I wanted to present you some of the methods of creating a passive income and also what kind of tools you can use to develop them.

As you see, sources of passive income greatly vary. This means that passive income can be obtained from almost any type of activity.

Receiving money regularly without the need to work day by day is a target worth working for because this leads you to financial independence and freedom. Passive income is a good perspective and I think everyone should try to do it.

As you saw, it is impossible to create a passive income without some investment in the form of money or time or both.

Mokokoma Mokhonoana, an African philosopher, social critic and writer said: "He who makes $25 000 annually through passive income is more enviable than he who earns $100 000 annually through a salary." I think these words can motivate many of you to start the action.

Sincerely, Donald Haskins

www.ingramcontent.com/pod-product-compliance
Lightning Source LLC
Chambersburg PA
CBHW070404190526
45169CB00003B/1102